Poems & Stories
{2016}

Poems & Stories
{2016}

Robert P. Parker, PhD

Poems & Stories

Copyright © 2016 by Robert P. Parker, PhD
Published by RoJo Press
Cover/Interior Design: Karen Hudson
Production Management: Janet Spencer King,
www.bookdevelopmentgroup.com

All rights reserved. No part of this book may be reproduced, stored in a retrieval system, or transmitted in any form or by any means, electronic, mechanical, or otherwise, without the prior written permission of the publisher, except for brief quotations in articles and reviews.

Printed in the United States of America for Worldwide Distribution
ISBN: 978-0-9972392-0-1

Praise for "Poems & Stories, 2016"

"In all of your poems, you are neither giving away too much nor too little. The emotion evoked by the poems (and for me) cannot be pinned down. I am familiar with the images created in each poem, but at the same time I am not. It is these poems/stories that connect to who we are. We are so simple yet so complex at times. We can feel so insignificant yet so precious and rare…Thank you for sharing your words with me."

—Jesse Silva, "Memoir for Christy (in press)"

"I loved 'Ralph' because of the ritualistic steps in enjoying a tomato, from washing it to taking the first bite as it bursts in your mouth. Most of all I loved the relationship and care and time that your grandfather had with you in the garden … 'But most of all I loved him for the pleasure he took in watching me.' What a great line…it wraps the entire poem into this simple sentence. I wonder if your grandfather knew how much it meant to you that he watched you enjoy that tomato. It is those small moments that prove that nothing is trivial. Everything counts."

—Jesse Silva, "Memoir for Christy (in press)"

"'Eva' was my favorite. Captured the essence of who she is and just put it out there for everyone to experience. Anyone reading that poem would want to meet 'Eva.' Period. Great stuff and nice to know you are back in business again! And 'Ralph' was awesome. Made me remember my grandfather and the things that I shared with him. Great times. It was the simplest things of those days that made life beautiful."

—Dirk Thomas

"'Eva' is…lovely. Heartfelt? Each of the poems has a particular grace, and grace may be a better word for me to use. Beautiful writing. I'm going to read and reread these poems."

—Judith Garry

"I love Bob's poem! It's so special. I will share this with my siblings. He captured Mom ('Eva') so well."

—Anita Landecker (Eva's daughter)

"I think you're a real poet, Bob. Definitely."

—Deena Linett, poet, writer of novels, short stories and essays

Dedication

To my friends and family who gave me the memories
floating through the imagination I have created
to be a writer and poet.

Contents

1: Poems

In the Wasatch Mountains	I
Finding a Poem, Thank You…	3
Response to "The Designers": A Short Story	5
Two Haikus	7
How I Write a Poem	9
Holes	11
Working	13
At the Brown Palace Hotel	15
Eva	17
Joyce: 1	19
Ruth Whitmore Parker	21
Ralph	23
Joyce: 2	25
After the Fact	29
Dad: 1980	31
Dad: 2015	35

2: Stories

The Bird Feeder	39
My Grandmother	43
Chris's Story	49

Foreward

I was Bob Parker's student at Rutgers University beginning in 1977, and I am honored to have been asked to write a foreword for Poems & Stories. The poems grew organically from some cherished and extraordinary experiences of his life and from great suffering—specifically, from the death of his son. As with the stories, they tell bits of a life and pieces about family and friends all these years later.

When I began at Rutgers, my first class was in English education with Professor Robert P. Parker. I was anxious, having come back to school after a number of years at home raising three children and having worked off and on at part-time jobs.

Professor Parker was easy and friendly, but I was intimidated by his fluent expertise in the classroom and by the rich and complex conceptual framework that was the subject of his course. The first question he asked that night was "What are we doing when we're teaching English?" Over time I learned that teaching English involved far more than correcting grammar. I saw also that I'd come into the discipline with no ideas of my own.

I remember his beautiful handwriting on the blackboard, which, over the course of the thirty years I've been teaching, I've mentioned to students dozens of times as my scrawl looped and meandered. I record this apparently superficial artfulness because Bob Parker was aware of esthetics as well as of the conceptual framework and history of teaching and the needs of his variously gifted—or hobbling—students. Everyone's been to school, so everyone—except the most gifted and rare teachers—seems to think that teaching is easy. That it is an outgrowth of serious consideration and intellectual flexibility over time is simply not included in most people's understanding.

Bob Parker is a consummate teacher, someone who has given many years to the understanding of what it means to learn and how a teacher can enable consequential learning. Parker "reads" his students with care, and his assignments keep them at what a psychologist-friend calls "the growing edge." After several courses in English education, Dr. Parker told me about an internship at a community college and said that I should consider applying for it. I remember exclaiming, "Oh, I couldn't do that!"

"Of course you can," he said, and so I did.

When we went back over those days some years later, I asked how he could have known I'd be able to handle that experience; I'd never taught, and my grad-school courses at that time were an ongoing act with the three children and my own radical changes. He said that he had seen something sturdy in me, a great gift that remains vivid all these years on.

We lost touch when Bob and his wife, Jo, traveled and moved, and I missed knowing where he was and what he was doing. One day—and I no longer know how I remembered that he might be in Nevada—I called information, got a phone number, and called it.

Jo, whom I'd known nearly as long as I had known Bob, picked up the phone and exclaimed, "Deena Linett, is that you?" I was so happy to have found them and deeply saddened to learn that Bob had had a stroke in 2009 and was still not fully able to talk, though he was writing and seeing friends and had been working in physical and other therapies for nearly five years. It was hard—and tiring—for him to talk on the phone, but we caught up, writing e-mails and sending each other what we were working on.

There's a poem in these pages, "In the Wasatch Mountains," that I remember from a read-around in grad school. Having grown up on the gulf coast of Florida and in the Northeast, I'd never heard of Utah's Wasatch Range. I remember that in an early draft of the work, a fishing rod appeared in the poem, but one student commented on the use of the word "rod," saying that it was phallic. (Freud had more currency in those days.) It's not here now, but the poem is full of beauty and appreciation for the natural world and for mystery, which Parker, whom I remember too simply as a big, apparently easygoing, confident man, makes familiar and explicit.

I love the complexity—there is so much heart and mind in his work, his teaching, his writing, and his life. None of that was apparent to me in those early days. I remain startled by my inability to recognize depth and range then, and surely Bob's ability to enlarge his best qualities has occurred over the years. Now, in these pages, the reader can find the weight and value of a deeply thoughtful, sensitive, generous, graceful, and kind person who knows adversity and can laugh and exclaim and remain active and take pleasure in his difficult life.

Deena Linett is the author of five books of poetry and a sixth due out in 2016, as well as essays, short stories, and two novels.

Everything that is made of love is alive.

—Anne Michaels, *The Winter Vault*

Poems

In the Wasatch Mountains

Aching legged,
I belly down in the
soft spring grass of a
high alpine meadow.

Below me, I can hear the constant
        rush-roaring
        of a snow-melt waterfall.

The stream is
        so clear that
I can see small rocks and
        rotting aspen leaves
        tumble along the bottom.

I drink quickly, feeling the icy water
        knife
        down to my stomach.
Breath-gulping, I lift my
        head
        toward the sun.

I feel cold drops run
        down my face.
My forehead is
        deliciously numb,
        and my lips tingle.

FINDING A POEM, THANK YOU...

Professor Skinner says that people
> *have poems:*

that events, experiences, circumstances
> accumulate
> to *form a poem*

that is *had like*
> a chicken laying an egg
> > or
>
> a computer disgorging a printout.

Forms, he says, are *predictable,*
> all programmed

by the personal histories of poets:
> no room for discoveries,
> personal shapes,
> or chance fusions—

no rubbing up against one another
> of sounds,
> > images,
> > feelings,
> > ideas,
> > *or dreams.*

Fie on you, Dr. Skinner:
> people find poems
> everywhere.

They dream them,
>   or shout them
>   or draw them
>   or glue them
>   or play them into shapes
no personal history could predict.

Sometimes, for a few moments,
>   interrupt your life to be
>   where children
>   or adults
>   find poems that you
>   could not imagine.

Response to "The Designer"

She began;
we listened.

Slowly, her story—
      sinuous,
      darting,
      all shimmering surface
      hinting at depth—
trapped us.

We listened harder, seeing
      the camel-colored woman,
      the designer with strong legs
      and bowed shoulders,
      the woman watching the parking lot,
      the designer's wife at parties,
and waited for release.
It didn't come.

Instead, we moved into
the designer's body,
      feeling his leg muscles,
      his frustration,
      his fears, and
      his small after-hours triumphs,
and half understood.

The story ended,
> abruptly.
> We were trapped,
> again.
This time in silence,
> with neck hairs prickling,
> nerves taut,
> bodies tense,
> still waiting for...
> what?

Two Haikus

Swooping V-winged tern
pauses, tucks, plummets wave ward
silver minnows flash.

Wild four-winged roses
open quiveringly wide
pink petals fall soon.

How I Write a Poem

First, I remove my glasses
    and
    close my eyes:
    in-sight is wanted here,
    not out-sight.

Next, I concentrate on the view
    in my mind's eye,
flipping images like slides
    in a carousel tray.
You could say that I conduct
    a mental dig:
    sifting memory shards,
    fragments of some sort.

I search for images,
    somehow,
    that are vivid,
    intact.

How do I recognize the fragments
that suddenly demand naming?
How do I know the right word when
    I find it?
The naming requires words
    to call forth, what—
    its beauty?
    its sadness?

Holes

You've seen the clam halves
    on the beach near the
    high-tide tangle:
bleached white, water smoothed,
    sometimes whole,
    sometimes splintered.

A few, if you've noticed, have
    small, round holes
    near the hinge.

Starfish made these holes:
    their legs tightly embracing
    the shell,
    their rasp-tongue drilling in
    to find soft stomach flesh,
    sucking out life.

That happens to people.

A kind of starfish wraps its legs
    around them,
    and a sharp tongue pierces their
    soft flesh.

Once ensnared,
they cannot escape that
    deadly embrace.

> I see them as a vision,
> > washed up,
> > misshapened,
> > ornamental,
> added to someone's collection
> > or slowly ground to
> > small, hard grains
> like the clams:
> > to build the shifting,
> > storm-shaped beach
> > > again.

Working

My son sits on his red swivel chair,
 one leg tucked under him,
 head tilted slightly to the right,
          drawing.

His hands move smoothly without hesitation,
          choosing a crayon,
          making a line or a figure,
          filling in spaces with color,
          blending one color with another,
until the picture is finished.

He seems to know just what he wants.
Sometimes he works for
          an hour
       getting the picture
          exactly
          right.

I like the finished pictures,
though I am tired of monsters and racing cars.
More than that, I like the quality of concentration:
 of patient,
 unhurried
 absorption
 in his work.

That's the key.

Periodically, his teachers tell me,
"His attention span is too short," or,
"He wastes time," or,
"He doesn't apply himself to his work."

I find it hard to tell them my image, but
it's harder for me to tell my son
> that I'd like to learn from him
> this way of working at things.

AT THE BROWN PALACE HOTEL

When the brunch was over and the check had arrived,
you said, "Sometimes you do things for those you love."

At earlier moments, made poignant now in memory,
we feel your love for us:
        a direct current,
        touching us again.

You gave yourself this way often, simply and directly:
        making the suggestion at a tense moment
            in our psychodrama,
        pointing our gaze to the deer
            that appeared outside your house,
        describing the flight of sandhill cranes
            outside your camper,
        admiring the painting of those cranes,
or talking about the book that you had nearly finished.

We will ask you for help,
        confident that you will give it in spirit
        just as graciously
        as you gave it in body.

        (with Josephine C. Mazzoli)

EVA

We sit in your living room
        high on the hill,
        sun setting,
        relaxed,
        wine in hand,
        listening to a story
        told by you.
Somehow, being there fits into your life,
        and ours too.
However, it is the laugh,
        underneath the story.

Eva's face lights up.
Her eyes glow.
Her laugh, quietly, breaks the silence.

It grows, slightly,
        for two or three heartbeats,
        and then it's silent—
        but not for long.

It is the most wonderful laugh imaginable:
        in the kitchen,
        in the dining room,
        in the bedroom,
        walking out to the pool,
        standing amid the orchids and fruit trees,
        or having a wonderful meal.

It only lasts a few seconds
    then quiet.
But it's wide ranging.

You have to listen carefully
    to her words,
    but only for a second.
Actually, people look at one another
    to see
    if she's joking.
And she is.
Then we laugh out loud
    because
    we want to be where she is,
    at that very moment,
    joined together.

Joyce: 1

I am four years old:
    Burlington, Ontario,
    the summer, and
    the front of the bungalow.

It was a long way out to Lake Ontario,
              and
at the center was the teeter-totter.

My mother placed my legs on the ground.
On both sides she placed my hands,
    and she said, "Hold on!"
    She got on the other side,
    high up,
    feet just hitting the ground.

We faced each other,
    she and I.
I, afraid and ecstatic.

Because I was small,
    she pushed me up,
    way high,
    pushed me down,
    pushed up higher
    until I was dangling,
    pushed down to the ground.

She pushed us up
        until
        I nearly fell
        but not quite.
Scared, but it thrilled me.

When we finished and
        climbed down,
she brought a pitcher of mint water
        to the table
        and cookies, freshly baked.
We sat and talked about nothing and everything.
        It was a happy time
                in her life.
For me, it was delicious.

RUTH WHITMORE PARKER

Your face, gilt framed,
has looked past me
      for years.
Often, I try to catch
      your eye,
mother of my father,
but you looked the other way.
Everyone likes you hanging
      In my foyer.
"Who is that woman?" they ask.
"Your grandmother?" they say.
"She's very beautiful."

Your pale, clear skin,
      upswept black hair,
      high cheekbones,
and faintly ironic smile
      invite my glance—
      and my questions.

Did you hold my father
 when he was a child?
Sing to him?
Comfort him when
      his father died,
      suddenly,
from the hemorrhage
  in his brain?

And who held you
> when you were sad,
> in pain,
> and dying?

Were you always serene,
> distant,
> faintly mocking?
Too elegant to be touched
> by anyone?

Ralph

With that look of amused attentiveness,
    Ralph watches me,
    twisting gently to the right,
    just as he had shown me.
I pick the ripe-smelling "big boy" tomato
from the drooping vine and cradle it in my hands,
    my fingers making small dents
        in its lovely, firm flesh.

He turns on the garden faucet
and washes the dust from the tomato
    and from the young boy's hand.
I shake the cool droplets from the fruit
    and take the saltshaker from
    his offering hand.

"You take the first bite," he says.

Carefully, I shake the white crystals onto
    the warm, still wet tomato.
Then, I bite into the acid-sweet, slightly salty
    flesh, juice squirting up my cheeks
    and dribbling down my chin.

I loved my grandfather for taking me to his garden
    and showing me how to pick his best
    sun-warm tomatoes.

> But most of all I loved him for the pleasure he
> took in watching me.
> That moment, with juice running down my face
> and dripping from my fingers,
> he knew it was the best moment in my life.

Joyce: 2

My mother was a beautiful woman:
    vivacious,
    carefree,
    smiling,
    spoiled, and
captivated by her presence.

I moved to Chicago.
We had a boy and a girl.
The girl was born just before
I started my doctorate.
I loved writing and reading
    but not grammar.

We arranged for my mother to come
    to Evanston
    for a visit
    with our week-old daughter.
I knew that she hadn't seemed well,
but I was thinking about
    the program.

I hadn't seen my mother
    since last summer.
I noticed the changes.
She thickened,
    aged,

wrinkles on her face,
but
in the back of my mind.

We welcomed her;
she was busy;
and
then she was gone.

A week later, I opened the sink:
eight bottles of
rye whiskey,
watered down,
at a different level.

I was devastated.
I called my Dad
but he laughed it off.
I was frantic,
so I studied harder.

Suddenly, one major heart attack
after Steve went back
to college.
I flew east.
I saw my mother when
she was in the hospital
for two months.

But I still hadn't gotten the idea
>that she would die,
>immediately.

She did, though.
She died in the downstairs bedroom,
>age fifty-seven,
>as though
>she slipped away.

After the Fact

Did you see us standing there
       by that hospital bed
      In Missoula?

You looked unmarked, normal,
sleeping deeply, and
       your heart beat
       as we caressed your arms,
       your warm chest,
       your long, red-blond hair.

A nurse came, soft eyed, and
       brushed your hair:
       carefully, lovingly,
 as if she were your mother.

 Did you hear us cry?
 Did you hear us say we loved you?
 And good-bye?

Finally, mute and drained,
       we wrenched ourselves
       from your bed—
       one by one.

 Did you feel them take your corneas?
 Did you know that a woman saw with
       your eyes?

What did you feel when they turned the
        machine off?

You were there in that hospital room,
and, later, in the Flemington church.
Where did you go?

Four years later, you came to that church
        in the rock,
        underground,
        in Helsinki,
        not speaking,
        to be with us.

You chose Matti, born one day before you,
        to be our guide.

You knew that his clear spirit
        would lead us there,
        just as you knew that
        one day,
I would understand why
you kept the card from Venafro
where the shaft of brilliant light
        from the icon
        in Jen's photo
        came from.

Dad: 1980

"Come to Waterford," he said.
    We did.
An alcoholic for thirty years.
He sobered up, again.

At the car,
    trunk open,
Dad said the first thing:
    "I'm glad you came.
    You and Jo.
    Together.
    I really am."
We picked up the bags
and walked to the house.

Later,
    frail,
    head thinning,
    potbellied
    but serene, now,
    sitting in the living room.
At seventy-five,
    he was still handsome.

He said,
    "I want you to know that
    I've finished everything
    on my list.

Five things: a line through every one.
I finished what I started."
A quiet smile on his face, he said,
"The last one was done
      not more than a week ago.
Printing as we speak.
In 1800, with Reverend Wooster Parker,
      and runs to 1980.
Only one ethnic name,
      yours,
      on the list.
And that's OK,
          now."
He handed me a manuscript,
      and I thought,
      "Well done."

He talked slowly about many things:
      down to earth,
      interesting,
      a glass of iced tea,
      sweetened,
      as he preferred it:
      comfortable
      in his chair.

Upstairs, we changed,
      came down,
      with towels,
      to swim.

Dad stood up,
>　　put on his hat,
>　　picked up his glass,
>　　walked out on his porch,
>　　sat in the rocking chair,
>　　to watch the swimmers
>　　and the ocean,
>　　ebb and flow,
>　　quietly.

We swam, dried out,
>　　sat in chairs outside,
>　　and talked and talked.
>　　Jo, silent, but listening
>　　to everything,

>　　　　　　now.

>　　Dad: alive and vibrant
>　　for the first time
>　　in more than twenty years.

I saw the tension slip away
>　　from his face.

Peaceful, I would say.
Jo witnessed it too.
>　　Indelible.

We kept it to ourselves.

Dad: 2015

First, touching my toes.
Then, slowly, upward
    to my knees.
To my Lower Dan Lien.
To my heart.
To my shoulders.
Finally, to my head.
This is where it began,
    always.

I saw a vision.
Each other,
standing there.
Broad smiles.
Dad walked toward me.
I waited.
Then, locked between
    each other's arms,
    hard,
    for a minute.
Stepping away slightly,
    we embraced each other
    on the shoulders.
Smiling broadly now.
I said my forgiveness to Dad.
He heard it.
Then he was gone.

Stories

The Bird Feeder

During World War II, my father clipped war reports from the New York Times, the Herald Tribune, and the Newark Star Ledger. He would cut out the reports and paste them methodically in a scrapbook. He never missed a day from Pearl Harbor to V-J day, labeling each scrapbook by month, by year, and by military campaign. By the end of the war, he had filled fourteen scrapbooks.

He built his bird feeder just as methodically, planning the size and shape and height of it to accommodate many different shapes of birds. I can still picture his meticulous hand-drawn design for the bird feeder, which was complete with arrows and numbers marking the dimensions, all done with a carefully sharpened hard-lead pencil. I can picture him at his workbench with its rows of tools on the wall in front of him, all neatly organized by category and by height within each category. With the design taped carefully just to his right, he measured and cut each piece of wood before assembling his bird feeder.

When he finished the feeder, he painted it just as carefully as he had assembled it: the roof was dark blue, the sides were beige, and he used off-white to touch it up. Then he cleaned the paintbrush with a putty knife, squeezing the excess paint off the paintbrush before wiping it with a clean cloth and hanging it on the wire to dry.

When the paint had dried, he hung the feeder on a crotch of the tree at just the right height for a sight line from a particular living-room window. Inside the window, he placed an easy chair angled carefully to give him an unobstructed view of "his" birds at the feeder. On a small table beside the chair, he kept two field guides to birds of northeastern North America so that he could read the titles from his chair. Beside the books sat two perfectly sharpened hard-lead pencils.

Beside the pictures, my father noted, in his precise, spidery writing, the exact time and date of each bird sighting. When he saw a new bird, he noted it in his field guide. I liked to look at the pictures of the birds. I tried to draw a few of the birds. But I could never understand how he could sit for hours, watching his birds at the feeder, or why he made such careful notes each time he saw a new bird.

He didn't belong to any bird-watching clubs, nor did he ever make field trips as other bird watchers did. He just watched from his chair and kept precise records. I don't know if he shared the pastime with anyone else, though he showed us the entries he made when he sighted new birds. During those times, he seemed as animated as I ever remember him being.

He was serious about feeding his birds, and I know the blue jays upset him when they chased the smaller birds away from the feeder, bullying them and hogging the food my father had so carefully put there for them. The blue jays were aggressive in an arrogant, strutting way, and my father wasn't. But as much as my father hated the blue jays, he hated the squirrels more. All the birds left when a squirrel came, and even the hardest taps on the window failed to chase them away. Sometimes they sat up, startled, but when he stopped tapping, they always began eating again within a few seconds.

Occasionally, when a squirrel came to the feeder, my father would get up from his chair and go upstairs to his study. I knew what he was going to do. From the top shelf in his closet, he would take down the Mauser .22-caliber rifle that his younger brother had brought him back from the war. Then he would open the bottom drawer chest that sat on top of his dresser. He would take out the box of shells, select two or three of them, close the box, and put it back in the drawer.

Then he would go upstairs to my bedroom window. He would open the window quietly; put one shell in the chamber; remove the safety, and, laying the barrel on the windowsill, take long, slow, careful aim at the squirrel. Then, squeezing the trigger slowly and deliberately, he would fire.

Before school, when I was nine years old, my father appeared in my bedroom carrying the rifle. I looked down from my window and saw the squirrel on his feeder. "Can I shoot this one? Please?" I said. "I've been taking lessons

with the rifle, and I can shoot pretty well now."
"All right," he replied. "Aim carefully, hold your breath, and squeeze the trigger slowly." My heart pounding, I took the gun and did as I had been taught. Squinting down the barrel through the notched sight, I aimed at a spot just between and just below the squirrel's shoulder blades. Slowly, I squeezed the trigger just as he had shown me.

Sometimes when he shot them, the squirrels would die without movement. At other times, they would be wounded and would skitter shudderingly, frantically down the tree and across the yard.

Occasionally, a squirrel would lurch straight up in the air then tumble to the ground, twitching then subsiding. This squirrel hardly moved. Its legs just spread out slightly as it sank down on the feeder. I put the gun down carefully, one shell ejected from the muzzle, and looked at my father. He smiled slightly. "Good shot, Son. Now we'll get the shovel and bury the squirrel in the woods." I smiled inside myself. I knew that we had to do it carefully because, my father said, squirrels sometimes carried diseases. I realized that I could sight down the barrel, aim directly at the squirrel, and shoot the squirrel because at age nine, I could do it better than my father could.

My Grandmother

When I was fourteen, my grandmother's bed was a foot from mine, on the other side of the wall. Whenever I woke up, I could hear her breathing from the other side of the wall: slow, uneven, labored, raspy. Occasionally, she would breathe a loud, long, shuddering breath like the one people are supposed to take in before they die. Each time I heard her breathe like that, I held my breath, waiting for her to breathe again. It seemed like minutes before she did. I lay there rigid, unmoving, frightened that I had heard what would be her last breath.

My two younger brothers slept at the opposite end of the house. If I heard her die, I would be the only one who knew she had. The thought terrified me. What would I do with that awful knowledge? Would I go into her room and try to wake her? Would I go downstairs and tell my parents? Or would I just lie there, trying to fall back to sleep, too afraid to move? What if she died, and I knew, but I was too afraid to do anything? When my parents found her dead the next morning, would they know that I had known all along? Would they be angry at me? Would they punish me for doing nothing? Or would they understand how terrified I had been?

I hated my grandmother for dying in the next room. It was bad enough that I had to visit her every day, not knowing whether she would recognize me. Not knowing whether she would talk to me. Not knowing whether she might make sense or mumble incoherently.

I never liked my grandmother. She had always been strange, disappearing into her room for days on end. She was "sick," my mother said, the whole time I knew her. "Don't you dare disturb her," they told us.

That was all right with me. I didn't want to see her anyway. She always had the curtain drawn, even on sunny days, and she always smelled funny, like a combination of medicine and a sour old-lady smell. And she read religious books. She went through every religion known to man: Christianity, Buddhism, Hinduism, Islam, and other varieties of religious practices and rituals. None of it seemed to do much good. The spells—or attacks—continued to occur.

When she was well, she wasn't much better. Just outside Bomma's kitchen was a small pump house: it was a lattice-walled enclosure with a roof, morning glories covering the walls, and nasturtiums growing all around the base. Inside was an old-fashioned cast-iron pump. We had to prime it with water and then pump hard. Shortly, icy-cold water would gush from the spout each time we pushed the handle up and down. We loved drinking the frigid water from the chipped gray-enamel cup that hung on a wall just inside the door.

But we didn't love having our heads held under the icy cold water or our mouths washed out with gritty, foul-tasting brown "Lava" soap. "L-A-V-A"—I can still hear the radio jingle. That is what my grandmother did when I swore. Since I was the oldest of six grandsons, I had to set an example for them. As a result, my mouth was clean, and my tongue was raw.

And that was only one of my grandmother's tricks. Just as she was death on swearing, so was she death on kids putting their elbows on the table while they were eating. If she saw an "offending" elbow, she would grab her fork and jab it in hard, sometimes drawing blood. I already hated her for the "Lava" soap taste in my mouth, and the tines in the elbow rubbed salt in the open wound.

One holiday, as everyone was sitting around the long table in Ontario, I got even. I was sitting next to my grandmother, where she could keep an eye on me, and I saw her put her elbow on the table. I grabbed the fork and stabbed it hard into her elbow, leaving four red marks, two with drops of blood emerging from them. Suddenly the table fell silent. Everyone watched my grandmother's face get redder and redder. At the other end of the table, my grandfather started to shake. He tried to make it look like he was coughing, but I knew better. He was laughing! His face got redder, and tears began to run down his face. Finally he grabbed his napkin, covered his mouth, and left the table.

He was gone for about ten minutes.

My grandmother just sat there. No one moved. My younger brothers and cousins looked at me in disbelief. No one said a word until my grandfather returned. Then the conversation resumed almost as if nothing had happened. No one punished me. No one even spoke to me, and my grandmother never, ever forked an elbow again.

I had turned the tables on my grandmother and had been protected by my grandfather. But now he had died, in Ontario, and she was turning the tables back on me—or that's what I thought. She was making me pay for all those years of plaguing her. She was getting her revenge by being ill again. But this time she was really dying, and this time I, who was afraid of the dark, was her keeper. And I couldn't tell anyone how I felt. I couldn't say, "I can't stand visiting her every day. I can't stand not knowing if she'll recognize me. I can't stand hearing her breathing at night, not knowing which breath will be her last. I don't want to take on this responsibility.

"I'm sorry for the fork in her elbow. I'm sorry I laughed at her for putting nasturtium leaves in her salad. I'm sorry for tearing down the sticky flypapers she hung in the kitchen. I'm sorry for making noise when she was ill. I'm sorry. I'm sorry!"

But I couldn't say any of those things. We didn't say things like that in the Parker family. I could only sit there, silent, waiting and listening for her to die. I didn't want her to die, but I did. I hoped that she would die when I was at school, wrapped up in my favorite novel. And she did. And they took her to Hamilton, Ontario. To rest in peace. I didn't go.

CHRIS'S LIFE

On January 1, 1979, when Barbara called to demand that Chris, at age fifteen, live with us forever, I asked Jo how she felt about that possibility. She agreed immediately, though she knew just how difficult our life would become. Chris struggled with his mother, his school, marijuana, and the law—but mainly with himself. He wasn't sure what he would do when he found himself. My commitment was to do everything in my power to turn his life around. And we did, giving unstintingly of our time, energy, and wisdom to him.

It was because of Jo that I learned how to be the kind of parent that Chris needed. Through those difficult times, Jo grew to love him like a son. When we stood by his hospital bed, she expressed her love and grief for him like a parent would've for her own child. Thank you, Jo, for giving Chris another caring and responsible parent and for playing such an important part in the happy, creative, friend-filled months before he died.

Chris knew he was going to die. Jo and I felt his grief after we arrived at the hospital. He worked on his art with new energy, saying, just before he died, that he had to work all weekend. That night, before his cerebral aneurism burst, he had arranged to have his friends cut his hair.

I have "A Dream Whilst Traveling" that Chris wrote for his creative-writing class. His friends call it a "spinning dream."

A Dream Whilst Traveling

We must be heading west. I am in the back of Morgan's pickup truck. It is a late-model maroon Chevy with a maroon corrugated-aluminum camp topper equipped with a hydraulically hinged back window out of which several colorful people slide, deliberately gleeful, and descend the grassy incline alongside the highway with their heads down as if on an Easter egg hunt. As a darkly clothed Indian woman and I climb out of the back of the truck, I notice the six or seven colorful people are playfully gravitating away from us and the back of the truck, and I experience a desire to join them. But the Indian woman has moved in front of me and to my right, and the shadows are in the form of a consistent smile of knowledge and intent, so I must do what she is showing me. She is resplendent. She stops mid-length along the truck, and I walk a foot or two past her and look out across the fields, which are the start of the ragged, protruding mountains. She indicates a spot above my head, and I

look up and see a metal cross made up of two three-foot perpendicular metal tubes. The ends of each tube are slightly bent toward the ground to accommodate two pairs of plastic handgrips, yellow on one tube, shiny red on the other. As I observe this floating device, she motions to a white sticker on the red grip with evident black lettering that seems to speak as I read it: it says, "Point the red handle to the big rock next to the sky."
I grip the bars and do so without a thought in my head. My body does not observe the laws of gravity and centrifugal force as I increase speed and rise upward, quickly disappearing from the scene altogether.

Our hearts burst with pain, and the tears streamed down our cheeks, but something incredible happened to us. Slowly, friends came to join us. They too wept and touched you. They shared their experiences with us. Chris had told his friends more about himself, his family, and his thoughts. Amid your art, they told us about the gentle, loving, creative, uplifting friend you had been to them. We saw a man who had expanded his life. Through your music and your art, your love and your spiritualism, you had become caring and giving beyond our imagining.

"I know of no more encouraging fact than the unquestionable ability of man to elevate his life by a conscious endeavor. It is something to be able to paint a particular picture, or to carve a statue, and so as to make a few objects beautiful; but it is far more glorious to carve and to paint

the atmosphere through which we look (Thoreau**).
Now that clear spirit and those memories live on in us. Thank you for the gift, which we will treasure. All of us are richer for it. We will love you and miss you always.

*Anne Michaels, *The Winters Vault*, Toronto: McClellan & Stewart, 2009.
**Henry David Thoreau, *Walden*, New York: Empire Books, 2013.

www.ingramcontent.com/pod-product-compliance
Lightning Source LLC
Chambersburg PA
CBHW070550300426
44113CB00011B/1859